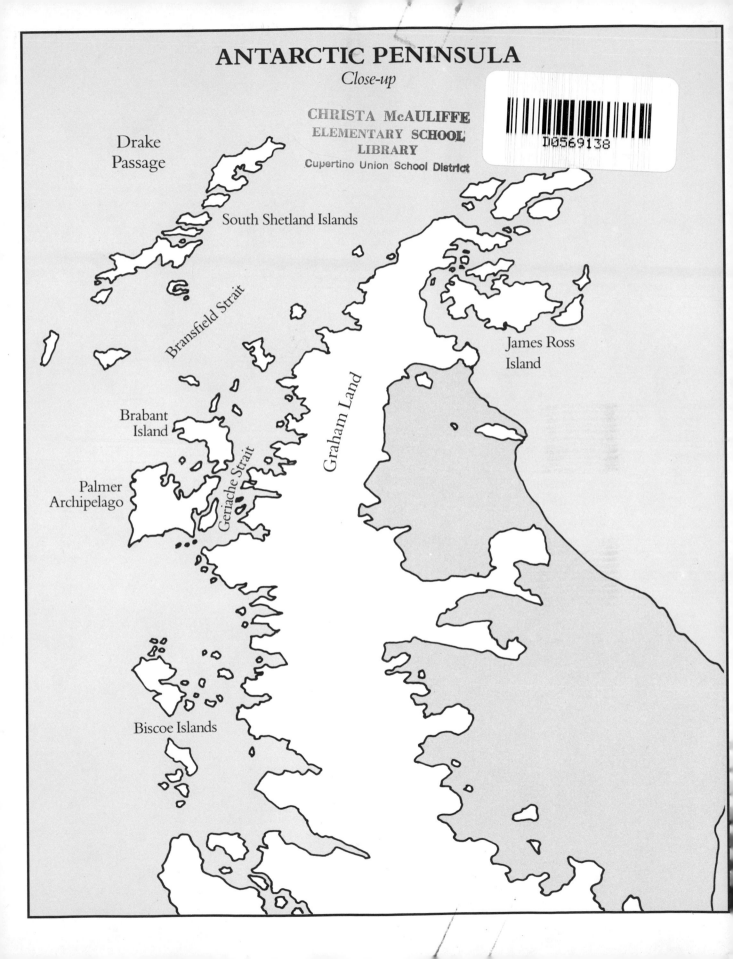

ANTARCTIC PENINSULA
Close-up

Drake
Passage

South Shetland Islands

Bransfield Strait

James Ross
Island

Brabant
Island

Graham Land

Gerlache Strait

Palmer
Archipelago

Biscoe Islands

Birds of Antarctica
The Wandering Albatross

Jennifer Owings Dewey

Little, Brown and Company
Boston Toronto London

This book is dedicated to

BRINTON C. TURKLE

First edition

Library of Congress Cataloging-in-Publication Data

Dewey, Jennifer.
    Birds of Antarctica. The Wandering albatross /
Jennifer Owings Dewey.
        p.   cm.
    Summary: Text and pictures take the reader
through a year in the life of Antarctica's wandering albatross.
    ISBN 0-316-18207-9
    1. Wandering albatross — Juvenile literature.
[1. Wandering albatross. 2. Albatrosses.
3. Antarctica.] I. Title.
QL696.P63D48   1989
598.4′2 — dc 19   88-31419
                                                              CIP

10 9 8 7 6 5 4 3 2 1

WOR

Published simultaneously in Canada
by Little, Brown & Company (Canada) Limited

Printed in the United States of America

CONTENTS

SOARING ON THE WIND

The wandering albatross, greatest of any modern
flying creature, cruises air currents over
turbulent southern ocean waters.
Aloft and soaring, the albatross flies with
graceful, tireless, gliding flight.
Balanced on long, narrow wings, the albatross
steers with its tail.

Soaring on the west wind,
this great bird flies out of the fog
like a ghost become real.

Other seabirds fade and emerge,
in and out of the fog.
The albatross, with a wingspread of twelve feet,
is the biggest.

Scaling down a wave until its wing tip seems
to touch water, the albatross rises in a long,
circular turn.
The bird's seventeen-pound body lifts and falls
in rhythm with the waves.

The albatross flying out of the fog is a female.
Dark feathers edge her spread tail and mark
the upper borders of her wings.
A large pink-white bill tipped with yellow
is sharply hooked at the end.
The bird's brown eyes are rimmed with gray eyelids.
Her feet are flesh-colored, tinged with blue.

For two weeks this particular albatross
has ranged over the sea, snatching fish and squid
from the waves with her beak.
Dropping and rising in continuous motion,
supported and carried by strong winds,
she conserves her energy by nearly effortless flight.
Wandering albatross have little need for sleep,
napping and resting on the wing.
Depending on the west winds to stay airborne,
the albatross is in harmony with wind and sea.

Wind speeds above the water are greater
than at wave surfaces.
Friction slows the wind on wave tops, sending it upward.
Taking advantage of this, the albatross flies
twenty feet above the waves, heading east
in skies half misty, half blue.

Warm air from the sea rising and flowing
into cold, dense air above, creates
updrafts and thermals.
Winds freshen.
The albatross wheels in circles,
banking on extended wings.
Were it not for westerly winds,
driven and shaped by the spinning of the earth,
the wandering albatross could not exist.
But the albatross, like other seabirds,
must return to the land to breed.

Skimming over blue waves sprinkled with shattered ice,
remains of a slab fallen from a glacier,
the albatross flies toward an island breeding colony.
Her nest is one of the nests in the colony.
A male albatross, her mate, broods a single egg
in the nest, waiting for her return from the sea.
Bits of ice floating on the water catch reflected light,
turning from white to robin's egg blue
and back to white.

HOME
The Antarctic Peninsula

Albatross nest in colonies on islands
off the coast of the Antarctic Peninsula.
The western edge of the peninsula is
fringed with islands.
Ice domes and permanent glaciers cover some of them.
Those near the northern tip are ice-free in summer.
Windswept headlands, gravel beaches, ice-cut platforms
of rock, ledges, and cliffs provide nest sites
for flocks of migrant breeding birds.

Migrations begin in late September and October —
winter's end in the southern hemisphere,
summer's beginning.
For the first time in seven months
the sun rises above the horizon.
Ice and snow melt off rocky island slopes,
sea ice breaks up, ice floes ride shimmery sea waves,
migrating cormorants, terns, and gulls
arrive from the north.

Penguins come.
Adélie, chinstrap, and gentoo.
Penguins do not fly like other birds.
Tobogganing on the ice, leaping and hopping
from the sea, walking up stony beaches,
trailing one behind the other, following well-worn paths
to rookeries used again and again —
penguins noisily mate and lay their eggs
in nests made of piles of stones.

Terns fly from the north,
gray backs, white stomachs, black-capped heads,
red bills and feet flashing across the sky.
Wilson's storm petrels flutter like swallows
on the waves, black legs and yellow-webbed toes
pattering on wave surfaces.

Wandering albatross settle on windy, rock-strewn slopes,
in nesting colonies used over and over,
year after year.

West of the islands
the southern ocean rolls with swells
traveling thousands of miles unchecked.
Winds blow over wave tops, making foam.
These winds are westerlies, named for the direction
from which they come.

The female albatross arrives from the west,
circling the island where her nest is and where
her mate is waiting. Fifty feet beneath her stretched wings
the island rises from a glittering sea.

Sunlight shines on beach stones.
A ridge of rock is the island's highest point.
The ridge falls away sharply to a slope of boulders and stones,
dotted with tufts of tussock grass.
The base of the slope flattens to a gravel shore
splashed with waves and studded with pieces of ice
stranded above waterline.

The female albatross flies in a wide circle,
sinking out of the sky with slow, easy motions.
Beneath her she sees penguins, all Adélies, all males,
gathered on the beach below the slope.
Close to shore, visible under water surfaces,
leopard seals swim up and down.
The penguins huddle nervously,
sensing danger in the water.

REUNION

Slipping through the air, the albatross loses altitude.
Webbed feet swing forward.
Landing high, near the ridge,
she walks down the slope.
Halfway down she folds her wings close against her sides.
Supple, fluid aerial control is lost
when the bird touches down.
She sways when she walks.

The albatross nesting colony covers two and a half acres.
Nests are three to six hundred feet apart,
leaving room for take-offs and landings.
Countless albatross feet trample the grass,
making runways and paths.
Albatross sit in their nests and face the wind,
white patches on a gray-green background.
Heads turn to watch the new arrival go by.

Giant petrels and fulmars nest on the slope.
A giant petrel, feathers looking stained,
circles and lands.
Petrel and albatross ignore each other,
one going up the slope, the other going down.

The sun looks ice-coated, a silver disk
in a cloudy sky.
Winds race around the island, ruffling feathers
on nesting birds, bending and shaking blades of grass.
In October, cloudy, cold days outnumber
bright, sunlit days.

While the albatross scans the slope,
looking for her mate and nest,
the penguins finally leave the beach.
A great thrashing and splashing reveals that
some are taken by leopard seals.
Skuas, Antarctica's birds of prey,
will pick and clean the remains
of unlucky penguins cast up on stony beaches.

Walking clumsily over uneven ground,
the female albatross reaches her nest.
In their ritual greeting
the albatross pair renew a memory.
In their gestures a lifelong bond is restored.

The female lowers her head to the ground.
Stretching to reach her, the male touches his bill to hers.
The pair touch bills over and over.
Leaning side to side, the female lifts and lowers
her head, wings partly raised.
Low moaning groans come from each bird's throat.
The sounds, like deep sighs, float away on the wind.

The male albatross is hungry
after fourteen days of sitting on the nest.
He lifts himself up, nudged gently by his mate,
stiff from sitting.
He stands on the rim of the nest,
steadying himself with lifted wings.
He turns and climbs the slope to the ridge top,
glancing back at his mate once or twice.
A few ungainly steps with wings raised
and the winds catch him,
bearing him away from the island,
over the sea.

The female albatross settles over the egg.
For two weeks she will brood the egg
and wait for her mate to return.

Wandering albatross live to be sixty or seventy years old.
Until they are six or seven they do not mate.
From age three on, young albatross perform
the ritual dance of courtship.
Until they are older the dance is
a discovery, a beginning.
With greetings and dances, young, unattached birds
form lifelong bonds that end only with death.

The young albatross of breeding age dance courtship dances, which are
followed by nest-building, mating, and
the appearance of a fertile egg.

The female albatross brooding her egg
on the island slope is seven years old.
It is her first egg.
Her mate, soaring over the sea,
is also seven years old.
Both birds were hatched on the island slope,
in nests still used by their parents.
The young pair built their own nest,
a nest they would return to, year after year.

One month earlier, when winter darkness was barely
broken by the sun's bright flash,
the young pair built their nest and mated.
Like other pairs in the colony, their mating took place
again and again, stopping only when the female
was ready to lay her egg.

A mating female presents her back to the male,
turning to face away from him, lifting and lowering
her head, pressing her wings to her sides.
She holds still, letting him know she is ready.
The male climbs on her back.

Using his wings to steady himself,
pushing on her neck with his bill,
he holds her under him.
His sperm travels through an opening called
a vent, or cloaca.
Entering the female's cloaca, the sperm
reaches the egg through a passage called an oviduct.
When it reaches the egg, the egg is fertilized.

A CHICK IS HATCHED

Two weeks after he flew away from the island
the male albatross returns, circling and
landing on the ridge.
The time is late December.
Walking with a tilting, swinging step,
the male albatross folds twelve-and-a-half-foot wings
against his sides.

The male nudges his mate from her place on the nest.
For a moment their round, white egg is exposed.
The egg is as big as an apple, smooth and white
but for a few dark speckles at the small end.
When her mate is securely on top of the egg, the female
walks up the slope to the ridge.
Before lifting her wings for flight
she looks back at her mate,
sitting on the nest, brooding their egg.

Every fourteen to eighteen days
the albatross pair exchange places on their nest.
Days of lowering cloud, driving sleet, and freezing winds
are days when both parents stay close to the nest,
close to each other.

After seventy-eight days
the albatross egg is ready for hatching.

When hatching starts, the female albatross is away,
feeding at sea.
Her mate is on the nest.
Under masses of glossy white feathers
the egg turns slightly.
A crack appears,
a struggle begins.

A more exacting time is difficult to imagine:
a tiny chick, shell-bound nearly eighty days,
not yet breathing air into its lungs,
hammers with its beak, forcing a way
free of a tough, resistant shell.

Inside the egg the chick has grown.
Simple clusters of cells have become heart,
lungs, bones, a circulatory system.
As an embryo curled in the shell,
nourishment came from a yolk connected to a cord.
The chick has absorbed oxygen drawn
through pores in the shell's surface.
Ready to hatch and leave the prison of its shell,
the chick tears the membrane lining the inside of the egg.
Air enters the chick's lungs for the first time.
The air supply is limited to a small amount
trapped between membrane and shell.
The chick must work fast to break through the shell
and reach outside air.

Twisting inside the egg, turning head over tail,
the chick presses against the shell, weakening it.

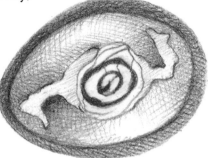

2 days after fertilization

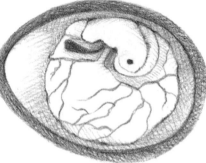

40 days before hatching

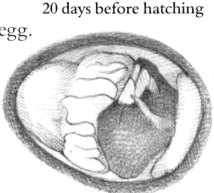

20 days before hatching

3 days before hatching

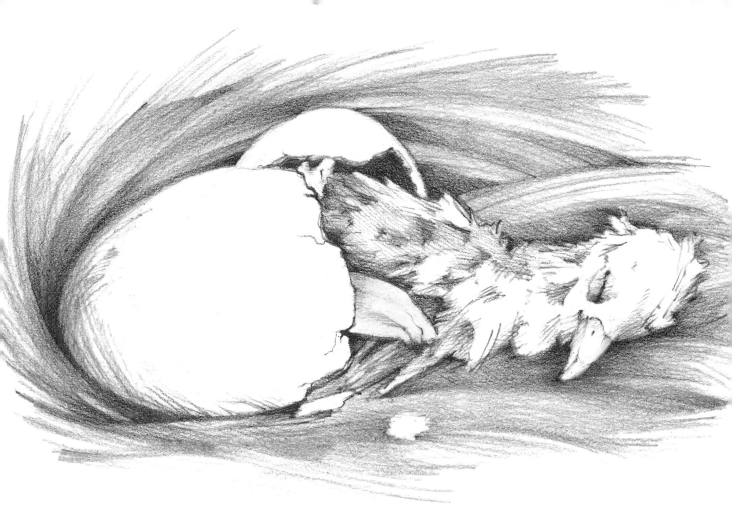

A day passes.
Inside the egg the chick struggles and strains,
a frail body convulsing with effort.
Nearly exhausting itself, the chick takes two days
to pull wearily out of the shattered remains of its shell.
Damp and shivering, it sprawls on a nest bed
of moss, lichen, tussock grass, stones, and mud.

The air is cold.
Shivering helps fluff the chick's down
and stimulate the flow of blood in fragile veins.
Dirty-looking down streaks the chick's
back, sides, and stomach.
Its eyes are squinted shut.
Tiny wings bend strangely, as if about to snap.
A stumpy white bill pokes out of a flat, unlovely face.

The male albatross lowers his head, pushing his nine-ounce
chick under oiled white breast feathers.
The first egg-free hours are spent drying
and resting, hidden out of sight.

Rapt and still, brooding with somber attention,
the male albatross settles over his chick.
His body is higher in back than in front.
A short neck and a head bigger than a swan's
support an enormous bill.
The male's dark, round eyes gaze out to sea.
Head, neck, and breast feathers are white-on-white,
textured like ermine.
Gray mottlings on upper wings blend
to black flight feathers edged with white.
Wings at rest, so great in extended length,
lie in three folds against the bird's sides.
Albatross have three bone segments in their wings,
rather than two, like other birds.
Wing sections tucked next to white-feathered breasts
are concealed under fluffed body feathers.
Long white wings project behind,
crossing over the tail.

Warming and protecting his chick,
the male albatross waits for his mate
to return from the sea.
Soundless and composed, perfectly still,
the albatross has the wind
and other nesting birds
for company.

MOTHER AND CHICK MEET

Returning to the nesting colony with a belly
filled with fish, the female albatross greets
her mate — and her new chick.

Climbing from the nest, the male albatross
gives the chick room to raise its wobbly head.
Staring with one eye and a cocked head
the female glares at the chick.

When the female was last at the nest
a round, white egg lay in the bottom.
Now the nest is littered with shell fragments,
downy feathers, and droppings,
and occupied by a dowdy-looking creature
trying to stand upright on spindly legs.
Uncertain but determined, the chick
stretches its neck, opens its beak
and stares back at its mother, eyes wide open.

"Cheep! Cheep! Cheep!"
The chick is hungry.

The male albatross stands close to the nest,
watching while the female lowers her head over the chick,
beak open, ready to deliver the first meal.
Half-digested fish and squid mixture, the
color of oatmeal, spills over the chick's head.
Some goes down the chick's throat.
The mother's first efforts at regurgitating food
end in splashed and spilled, ill-smelling fish soup.
Dropped food is quickly scooped up by sheathbills.

Sheathbills are notorious scavengers of the nesting colony.
They have chicks of their own to feed,
stashed in messy nests of bones,
feathers, rotting food, and stones.
Albatross pay no attention to sheathbills,
who go about their business undisturbed.

HIGH SUMMER
The Growing Chick

Ten days after hatching, the chick sprouts
a new coat of down — thicker and fluffier than the first.
Sitting and staring with bland, round eyes,
the chick swells and fattens with every meal.

The parent albatross continue to feed their chick —
making trips to the sea more frequently
to keep up with the chick's ever-increasing demand for food.
The chick grows quickly,
more than doubling its weight in two weeks.

January and February — midsummer along the edge
of the Antarctic Peninsula — bring day after day
of cloudless skies stretching over a sea as smooth as glass.
Ocean swells rise and fall with gentle, soothing motions.

Storm petrels emerge from nests in cracks of rock,
fluttering in busy flocks over the sea.
Delicate black beaks peck at tiny organisms
floating near the water surface.
Chunks of ice ride the swells.
Sunlight bounces off glacier shores and icebergs
as big as the state of Rhode Island.

Soil on the slope is slick and slidey,
saturated with moisture.
Elephant seals, coated with slippery black mud,
heave in and out of wallows, laboring up and down
the island's slopes.

The albatross chick sits in the nest and grows.
The chick's world is the nest —
for a year the chick will know nothing
of the world beyond the nest.
Regurgitated food slips down its throat,
parental feathers press warmly, protectively,
around it.

Other albatross chicks in other nests
are fed and tended by their parents.
The chicks keep to themselves, never leaving
the high, mounded ridges of their nests.
On quiet, windless days the cheeping and murmuring
of albatross chicks is a faint sound floating
on the cold air.

Gradually the parent albatross slack off feeding.
Winter is coming — summer's end is near.
By March the albatross pair come and go half as often.

Ten inches tall, round, firm, and fully clothed
in ample layers of thick, curly down —
the chick looks like a pumpkin with feathers and eyes.

WINTER ARRIVES

In March, Antarctica's winter begins.
The chick, left alone more often,
for longer periods of time, is safe.
No enemies frighten or disturb the tranquil,
unaware albatross chicks sitting in their nests.
A penguin wandering off track, stumbling
across an albatross nesting colony,
is driven off by a foul-smelling liquid
squirted out of tube-shaped nostrils.
The liquid is both stomach gas and half-digested food.
Even tiny chicks have this skill: they are able
to drive off any bird attempting to bother them.

Gull-like skuas fly over penguin rookeries,
terrorizing parent penguins, dark wings spread,
golden hackles raised.
The skuas seize penguin chicks in beaks and talons,
dragging them across rocks, tearing them apart.

Penguins have few ways to fight
heavy-bodied aerial attacks.
With their size, and using smelly stomach gasses,
albatross defend themselves and their chicks.
Their size saves them.
Over millions of years skuas have learned
which is the easier victim.

When albatross chicks are most vulnerable,
alone in their nests, it is winter.
The skuas are gone.

Winter winds and storms come,
swallowing the island in mist and frozen clouds.
The sun, so dazzling four weeks earlier,
is poised at the horizon, ready to sink
and vanish out of sight.
Antarctica's summer ends.
Winter begins.

The chick's mother and father leave the island together.
Walking to the ridge top, lifting their wings to darkening skies,
letting the wind reach under them and carry them away.
Tucking webbed feet under spread tails,
long narrow wings supporting them,
the albatross pair drift from the island,
away from the nest and the chick.

On the beaches of the island penguins stand
under rock ledges, finishing their molts.
Penguin chicks have left for the sea —
where they spend the months of winter darkness.
Terns, skuas, giant petrels, and cormorants migrate north.
All the summer's crop of chicks are out of their nests —
all but the albatross.

Albatross are so huge and live so many years,
it takes a long time for them to grow.

When Antarctica's winter darkness has fallen,
all the penguins are gone.
Piles of discarded penguin feathers
are the only sign they were ever there.
Rookeries are buried in snow.
Rocky paths are covered with ice and snow.
Sea ice spreads, first a sheet thin enough to see through,
and grows to a thickness of seven feet.

The chick sits, woolly and fat,
alone in a snow-encrusted, untidy nest pile,
able to see nothing in the darkness.

Silence falls on the colony.
A few muted sounds come once in a while —
the faint, irregular cheepings of albatross chicks.
The chick's parents are now gone,
soaring over a dark, wintry sea.
From time to time throughout the long winter,
albatross parents return to the island
to feed their hungry chicks.

THE STORM

In late June the albatross pair are flying together,
soaring over the sea, feeding on fish caught in the waves.
The birds take turns going back to the island.
First the male, then the female,
turn on wings nearly touching icy wave tops,
flying off into dismal, black skies,
returning to their chick.

They separate and pair up again.
Together, and with others of their kind,
they range over the wildest, stormiest
ocean waters on earth.

Mantles of fog condense and rise on the water,
turning darkness even darker.
Seabirds sweep low over the waves,
half-invisible in the shadowy world of Antarctic winter.
In the southern hemisphere June is a time
for savage storms.

Suddenly the albatross pair become trapped
in a storm of special violence.
They fight buffeting, battering winds,
gales carrying pellets of ice and snow
across hundreds of miles of ocean.
Wind and sea join in a roaring, tumultuous, howling union.

The male albatross, losing stamina, somehow finds
his strength is not enough — he feels himself slacken.

In the turmoil of the storm he searches for his mate.
He cannot find her.
He sees nothing.
Around him the air is frozen and white —
a blind blur of storm.
Seas swirl to seventy feet, then a hundred.
The bird's determination dwindles and declines.
He soars to the tops of waves, drops in the troughs,
using all his strength to hold steady
and beat the wind.

The albatross is fighting the west wind,
a wind that blows around the world continuously,
around and around, forever.

The great male albatross cannot win the battle.
As if charged by electricity, the exhausted bird
makes one last, agonizing effort to remain alive.
Stretched wings, flexed in the wind, weaken and grow weary.
Stomach and breast muscles fail.
Eyelids close over round, dark eyes.
The huge bird falters, and his faltering is fatal.
Black seas reach up to claim him, to consume him,
to swallow him in cold, wet, final darkness.
He is lost.

Six hundred miles away, on the edge of the storm,
the female albatross swoops down to catch a squid
drifting on the surface of the sea.
Stormy, windblown seas have driven low-depth animals
to the surface.
The meal, so urgently needed, so abruptly taken,
saves the female albatross from death.
New energy, fresh will, surge in her body.
She survives.

Lifting itself up from a nap,
the chick shakes downy feathers
glistening with snowdrops.
A light appears in the sky.
At first so faint it hardly seems real,
the light slowly spreads and climbs.
It is the sun — returning from the north
to brighten Antarctica's ice-bound
shores and seas.

FIRST FLIGHT

Hunger grips the chick.
Stomach muscles contract and cramp with emptiness.
The chick's last meal was taken weeks earlier.
The chick's strident cheepings are joined
by other chicks calling for their parents
and for food.

It is November, the beginning of summer's first light —
some chicks have not survived winter's darkness,
the bitter cold, and infrequent feedings.
Some chicks lie dead in their nest piles.

Ice and snow melt from the island slope,
exposing beds of moss laced with ice crystals,
pads of lichen the color of dead leaves,
and gray rocks stained with bird droppings.
Sea ice breaks up, floes crash against one another,
leads of blue-black seawater open.
Penguins return, noisy and quarrelsome in their rookery.
Leopard seals patrol the shores.

The chick's mother circles the island
on her great wings.
Glancing down she sees penguins,
busy in their rookery,
lingering on stony beaches.

Dropping lower she makes a wide sweep of the island.
Landing near the ridge top, she nearly tumbles
head over tail when her feet touch the ground.

The mother albatross regurgitates a hefty meal
of squid and fish down the chick's waiting throat.
The meal follows a long period of fasting.
It settles like a stone in the chick's middle.
The chick, almost a year old, is changed.
It now looks like an albatross.
Dark brown feathers, no longer fuzzy down, cover its body.

Brown all over, except for a white face and throat,
the chick has grown. It weighs seven pounds
and has a wingspread of five feet.

Around the chick and its mother, albatross pairs
greet each other, lifting heads and touching bills.
The female albatross engages in no ritual greetings,
no courtship rite. She has no mate.

Albatross chicks in their first summer
out of the nest all look alike.
Wandering over the slope, calling with low,
humming voices, they experiment
with the wind under their wings.
Still fed by their parents, spending
long hours asleep in their nests,
they slowly gain strength and independence.

All albatross parents who have chicks
wait a full year before mating again.
The care and feeding of one chick is enough.

The mother albatross follows her chick around the slope.
She follows it up to the ridge top.
By midsummer the chick wants badly to fly.

First tries end, again and again, in forced landings,
somersaults, and crashes on the lower part of the slope.
Sometimes the young bird drops out of control
into a crowd of jostling, squawking penguins
standing on the beach.

Other young birds try their wings,
practicing aerial skills.
Rolling and pitching on stony ground,
albatross chicks learn the hard way.
Finally, after many tries, the young albatross flies.

Walking to the ridge top, running with bouncing step,
the young bird's upraised wings are caught by the wind.
This time nothing goes wrong.
The young bird soars over the edge of the island,
wings spread, tail feathers wide, webbed feet tucked under,
lifting into a bright, Antarctic summer day.

LIFE ON THE WIND BEGINS

Albatross need time to grow.
For two years the young albatross will soar
over wild and stormy seas, never touching land.
With wings bowed and flexed, it will ride out hurricanes.
When winds die, it will settle on smooth waters,
bobbing and floating, waiting for the winds to rise.

The young bird will feed from the sea —
snatching fish and squid from the waves with its hooked beak.
Flying on westerly winds, the young albatross
will circle the earth, napping and dozing on the wing,
traveling the ocean's span, three thousand, three hundred ninety-seven miles.

Alone, or in company with other seabirds,
the albatross travels in the direction
of its departure from home ground.
Albatross fly with the wind, around the world,
knowing the wind will bring them back.

Two years from the time it leaves the island,
the young albatross finds its way home.
The albatross returns to the same island,
the same slope, where it was hatched.

42

In play, in preparation for adulthood,
and to establish a bond,
the albatross will dance courtship dances
and ritual greetings.
In six or seven years
the albatross will build a nest with its chosen mate.
An egg will appear, and a chick will be hatched.

Every spring this young bird's mother
returns to the island nesting colony.
An albatross mates for life.
So when a mate is lost, it takes time to find another.
Three years after the storm at sea left her
without a mate, the female will dance
a courtship dance with a new mate.
An egg will result,
and a new chick will hatch.

Until then the female albatross continues to circle
the southern ocean, from the arrival of winter darkness
to the return of summer's light —
soaring on the west wind.

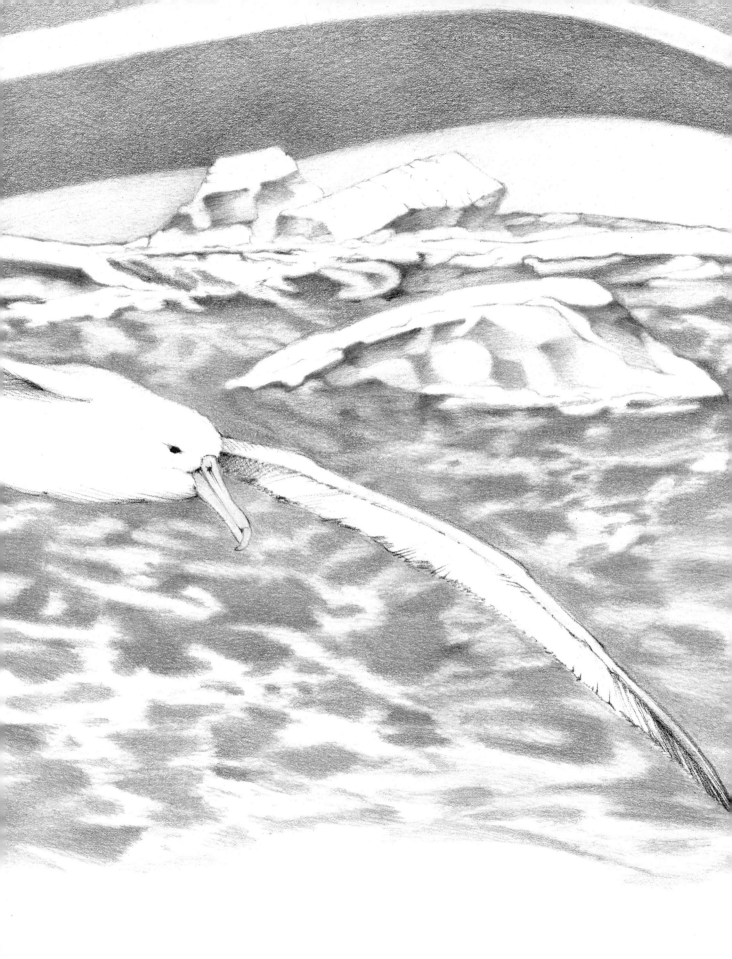

GLOSSARY

Adélie penguin
The Adélie penguin is one of eighteen living species of penguin. Penguins are flightless birds adapted for life on land and in the sea. Penguins live in the southern hemisphere. The Adélie and Emperor penguins live farther south than any other bird species. Because they are well insulated with layers of fat and dense plumage, penguins are able to survive the extreme cold of the Antarctic region.

Albatross
Albatross are members of the petrel family of seabirds, a large and diverse order distantly related to penguins. The wandering albatross is the largest of any other albatross, and the largest flying creature on earth. The wings of a wandering albatross are long and narrow, sometimes with a span of thirteen feet.

Antarctica
The seventh continent, Antarctica, lies at the southern tip of the world. A huge mass of land covered with ice, Antarctica is as big as Europe and the United States combined. It is the coldest, windiest, and iciest place on earth.

Cloaca
Also called a vent, the cloaca is the single opening in a bird through which sperm, eggs, and the bird's droppings all pass.

Down
Down is the first plumage of birds, a fine, thick mat of feathers growing extremely close together. Down is shed and replaced by adult plumage when a chick matures.

Floe
A mass of floating packed ice, usually more than nine feet across.

Fulmar
Fulmars are large-to-medium-sized petrels. Fulmars have strong, sturdy bodies and heavy bills. Their tails are short and square-cut. In strong winds fulmars flap and glide, able to fly skillfully through the worst Antarctic storms. Fulmars breed on coastal beaches and islands in the southern hemisphere. They feed by scooping fish, plankton, and krill from the tossing waves of the sea.

Glacier
A large mass of ice formed by compacted snow. The weight of a glacier can force it to move. Ten percent of the earth's surface is covered by glaciers.

Hackles
The long, slender feathers at the necks of some birds are called hackles. A bird raises its hackles when frightened, excited, or attacking.

Iceberg
A large, floating mass of ice broken or fallen from a glacier or ice shelf. Icebergs are often of tremendous size and sometimes take five or six years to melt into the sea.

Migration
The movement of birds or other animals from one region to another is called migration. Migration commonly takes place at a change in season.

Petrel

One of the largest orders of seabirds, petrels range in size from as tiny as a sparrow to as big as a turkey. All petrels fly. These seabirds have dense plumage, webbed feet, hooked bills, and a pair of curious tubular nostrils. All petrels lay a single egg and take longer than other birds to raise their young. Petrels live a long time, some as long as fifty years. The wandering albatross is a member of the petrel family of seabirds.

Regurgitate

The return of partly digested food from stomach to mouth is called regurgitation. Many birds and other animals feed their young by regurgitation.

Skua

Skuas are large, gull-like birds with dark plumage, a gray-black bill, and black, webbed feet. The skua is called "the eagle of the South Pole" because of its ferocious attacks on penguin chicks. Skuas also prey on other chicks in other nests in breeding colonies in the Antarctic.

Southern Ocean

The region of the world where the Atlantic, Indian, and Pacific oceans converge is called the Southern Ocean. It is this ocean which surrounds Antarctica.

South Pole

A geographical place, an imaginary place, marking the southernmost spot on earth.

ANTARCTICA
Overview

Atlantic Ocean

Indian Ocean

Weddell Sea

Ronne
Ice Shelf

● South Pole

Ross
Ice Shelf

Ross
Island

Ross Sea

Pacific Ocean

☐ *Southern Ocean*　　　☐ *Permanent Coastal Ice*　　　☐ *Antarctic Continent*